A COLLABORATIVE POETRY COLLECTION

Edited by

Dasha Kelly Hamilton

Wisconsin Poet Laureate

© 2025 copyright Jaded Ibis Press

First Edition. All rights reserved.

Printed in the USA. No part of this book may be used or reproduced in any manner without written permission from the publisher, except in the case of brief quotations embodied in critical articles or reviews. For information, please email: info@jadedibispress.com.

No part of this book may be used or reproduced in any way for the training, development, or operation of artificial intelligence (AI) technologies, including generative AI technologies. The rights holders expressly reserve this publication from the text and data mining exception as per Article 4(3) of the Digital Single Market Directive (EU) 2019/790.

ISBN: 978-1-938841-37-8

Book design and illustrations: Nicole Roberts

This book is available in paperback and electronic book format.
Hamilton, Dasha Kelly

A Line Meant / Hamilton

TABLE OF CONTENTS

Forward   1

Every Distance Seemed like an Opening   5
    DISTANCE Collective   6
    Close Call   8
    The Opening   10
    BLAX   11
    Looping Intersections   13
    Untitled   14
    Freedom's Lament   15
    en route   16

The Cool Water Is Hard to Gulp Down   17
    GULP Collective   18
    Quit Running In & Out   20
    my grandmother, a lake   22
    Untitled   25
    Meeting at the River   26

Untitled	28

Somehow Seems like Yesterday's Rain — 29
RAIN Collective	30
Retirement	32
That time Lily left Marshall to follow her dreams of being an artist	33
creative wash	34
Like Yesterday's Rain	36
Somehow, Seems like Yesterday's Rain	37

In the Bough of an Anxious Frenzy — 39
FRENZY Collective	40
American Happiness	42
On So Many Levels	44
November 17th, 2016	45
Untitled	46
from the boughs tossed in anxious frenzy	48
A Bouquet of Regret	50
Silhouettes	54
Misunderstood	55
Untitled	57

And Holy Hot Damn, the World Is Suddenly Something Different — 59
SUDDENLY Collective	60
Blue Bird	62
Changes	68
Too Much!	69
Search	71

Untitled	73
Suddenly Something Different	74
Psalm 1	75

Roots Are Tough as Dreams — 79
ROOTS Collective	80
Field Guide	82
My Poem	83
Dedicated to Ms. Dasha	85
Throwing Ropes	86
Roots	88

A Canvas Full of Ocean and Song — 89
CANVAS Collective	90
From a Door Worth Opening	92
Sand Etchings and Pesos	93
When We Were	94
In Another Language	95
Beach Walk	96
Art Attack	97
Dive In	98

Old Rhythms Find the Hands — 101
RHYTHM Collective	102
Manoominike-giizis	104
Skipping Records	105
The Children's Hour	106
Mouldwarp	107

Once Sweet with Aging Pears and Autumn Breezes — 109
    PEAR Collective — 110
    Still Life — 112
    Transformation — 113
    Burnt Amber — 114
    Once Sweet with Aging Pears — 115
    Orchard — 116
    Once Sweet with Aging Pears — 117

Unfurl, like Petals Longing to Bloom — 119
    UNFURL Collective — 120
    New Dimensions — 122
    This Year I Alone Went — 123
    A Mirage — 124
    Untitled — 125

Forward

One line of poetry can work like a spell, conjuring a memory for one person and pulling gospel from someone else. Every poem and story glimpses the many ways we love, fight, heal, and explore. Every one, a gift.

My lifework as a writer, performer, and creative change agent affords a spectacular view of the human landscape. As Wisconsin Poet Laureate, I wanted to share this dynamic experience. I launched the *A Line Meant* project to have poems stitch us a little closer together. Single lines of poetry served as monthly prompts for new poems and fresh discussions. The project included a broadcast dialogue series and a statewide poetry exchange.

Imperative to the project design was the inclusion of writers who reside in prison facilities. Of all my outreach work—impacting thousands of youth, curating hundreds of events, coaching scores of organizers, collaborating with countless creatives—teaching in carceral spaces has been my absolute favorite. I get to encourage and empower people to shape their own sanctuary, one poem and one story at a time.

The *A Line Meant* anthology presents selected works from fifty-nine poets, hailing from thirty-six cities across my home state. The project invited the creativity of neighbors and connected the humanity of strangers. The resulting collection includes poems from poets laureate, inmates, farmers, servers, retirees, professors, parents, veterans, sports fans, students, nurses, and a host of lives in-between. Together, in poetic conversation, the work glimmers with the unexpected gorgeousness of neighbors. Every one, a gift.

Dasha Kelly Hamilton

A NOTE ON *A LINE MEANT*'S STRUCTURE

Each section starts with a collective poem. Random lines were pulled from random poems submitted under each prompt and assembled into a new poem. The attributions for each line are cited at the bottom of the page. Each of these "found" poems created by Dasha precedes the original works that served as inspiration for each section. Following similar iterative and generative processes at every step of the anthology's creation, it is hoped that the line between professional and hobbyist poet is blurred, and new, powerful art is birthed from the margins.

Every Distance Seemed like an Opening

DISTANCE Collective

I walk out into the deep water
And still voices are circling around
to bind us all to the place where stars are born.
You are the distance that allowed us to become
  more intimate.
Did you know you helped write the music for these
  words
and will always be there?
Can we not share space
brave the elements
be caressed by the Sun's last light touch, blue-gray
  with hues?
Maximizing my potential
because life is such a bumpy road.
If only we had known.

Angela Hoffman, Jefferson
Alfonzo Washington, Plymouth
Erin Schneider, La Valle
Joseph Cook, Oregon
Matthew McDonnell, Waupun
Mario Willis, Milwaukee
Marilyn Zelke Windau, Sheboygan Falls
Cristina M. R. Norcross, Oconomowoc
Donnie Gilchrist, New Lisbon
Samuel White, New Lisbon
Charles Payne, Madison
Thomas Cannon, Oshkosh

Close Call
Dana Maya, Madison

When the pandemic came
the doors of the houses
closed / then the restaurants
closed / the doors to the schools
closed & the shops & salons
closed / then the places that never close
closed. We went home took off our real
clothes put on pajamas & sitting
close, read the news. It said not to
stand
too close the space prescribed was
—6 feet—
but every distance
seemed like an opening
it filled with our longing
we couldn't stop
looking at each other
as we always had but more now
averted eyes, downcast
walking the bike path we held
our breath as we passed
we wanted to know
strangers, we thought about
strangers every night as we read
we were good citizens
we washed our hands
we thought about bodies

& missed all the people
we knew & didn't know
The distance is closeness; it's
proximity. It's danger or it's safety or
it's love or sickness
or if not—it's a
close call.

The Opening
Lisa Vihos, Sheboygan

When I was young,
every distance seemed like an opening.
First there was a road,
then a door, then a keyhole.

With each opening,
the world got smaller
and I wondered how
I would get to the other side.

Now that I am older
I can look back and see
it is in the passage
that the opening becomes clear

and that each time I slip
from one hole to another,
the key that I search for
is right here in my hand.

BLAX
Adebisi Agoro, Milwaukee

Every distance seems like an opening
And my hope again
Was not to get caught on the ropes
again
Entangled like Jada
Or strangled by fallopian
While I dance with the devil
In this disco quite dystopian
Utopia was a mere hope
For broken men
No country for cowards
Unaccepting of criticisms
As stated by Andre 3000
"My soliloquy makes it hard
For some to swallow"
But so is cod liver oil
The silver sliver that bursts
The pulsing boil
Exposing truths in hues
That leak like pus & blood
My people's the type
Who got it out the mud
Digging way past six feet
Deep
A passage is what we seek
Or in other words
An opening.

 *The app called with the prompt to write. I simply answered the call.*

Looping Intersections
Thomas Cannon, Oshkosh

Life begins today and stretches out
Like a stage whisper, like a heavy fog
Which is why now matters.

There was a time, long ago
When our visibility was infinite
Yet didn't we still white knuckle it?
The horizon, too far away
Was slow-motion panic.

Each day more roads appeared
Every distance seemed like an opening
At those ever-looping intersections of fate
We might step off in any direction
We feared every direction was wrong
When every direction was right.
If only we had known.

Untitled
Alfonzo Washington, Plymouth

Every distance seemed like an opening
Like traveling and discovering a vacant lot
Not one occupant, it's empty
Even in the fullness of its life
It seemed alone from every distance
Like an opening with no one invited but you
A whisper in the distance
Echoed within your ears
Who's there?
The sound of wind whistling
In the vacancy of this abandon
Feeling like a bandit that broke in
To an opening
You saw a sign in the distance
Instantly read with no resistance
Population zero: a ghost town
Still voices circled around
Surrounding emptiness
It seemed like an opening, then, a realization the door was locked
Even with the right key in the keyhole, no entrance
Looking into the window
In the reflection stared back a Black Man
Surrounded in Americanism

Freedom's Lament
Donnie Gilchrist, New Lisbon

Could You speak to Love about my hate for Hope?
How does one escape and cope with a fixed timeline
so out of line with my atrophied soul?
I have seen the fracture of the human soul,
pieces healed and then unnoticed.
Sitting in the wrong room right next to you,
I wonder when you'll acknowledge me.
I am the You that you aspire to be.
I am the lost and left-behind vestige of truth
You never believed in. I am the question,
the answer, and the reason.
You are strongest at the best and worst of times,
weak when the days end, hopeless and alone at night.
A night I rail against, for covering up everything that's exposed
beneath the sun, like trees blooming under clouds free to be
caressed by the Sun's last light touch, blue-gray with hues
and undertones that Nature proves possible.
Subtle hints of smoky orange and cotton-candy pinks,
the reflection of Hope's dreams that shatter against
the rocks of Reality.
Broken. So close I choke on the end of each sentence
before it has begun, like a song unsung by the Prisoner.
After Hope leaves you waiting for the train that will never
    come,
I see me in you when Bitterness and Hate blind everyone.
Every day you get up and face Oblivion with courage,
killing me slowly, as every distance seems like an opening.

en route
Mario Willis, Milwaukee

with his thin shoulders he waits.
a child of the depression
he forgets the past behind him.
promises you another home
a better job
new friends.
carved out by generations
a living made of asphalt and concrete.
he can't tell your secrets & wouldn't
dare judge your companions.
wouldn't tell you where to get off
and will always be there
when you want to go home.

The Cool Water Is Hard to Gulp Down

GULP Collective

I once heard patience builds progress.
Sacrificial, as every daughter heard
unrelenting ghosts of pain, disappointment, and
*   heartbreak.*
Life, an endless series,
but oh, how good it tastes
carrying a desperate heart, a muddled mind.
Our pulses are the waves of life
if we want to stay alive.
I love the person I have come to see
as if I ain't got my own set of eyes.

Joseph Cook, Oregon
Tyler Odeneal, Milwaukee
Terran Kess, Redgranite
Lisa Vihos, Sheboygan
Cristina M. R. Norcross, Oconomowoc
Angela Hoffman, Jefferson
Fontaine Baker, Winnebago
Charles Payne, Madison
Angelica Munsell, Union Grove
Samuel White, New Lisbon

Quit Running In & Out
Karen Middleton, Milwaukee

You're letting the flies in. And don't let the door slam.
Out you go. We pull weeds around tomatoes,
feed chickens, hang upside down from clothesline poles,
run through cool stiff sheets that smell of sun,
ride Smoky and Maverick to the tank to watch frogs,
and to the creosote pole where we put our ears
against the rough and hear a telephoned hum
that travels thousands of miles. The world is big.

But that heat dries us, tires the horses,
and cactus barbs can't be pulled out straight.
Lunch waits for us back at the house,
and after Momma's kind-of siesta, library books
whose hardbound but soft pages smell
of glue and ink, hold surprises and
hidden heroes, painted in watercolors
as they were meant to be. We become drowsy.

Sleep glides from our spines to our
shoulders then to the fronts of our eyes,
deep but quick. After we wake, neighbors
come over. We climb mesquites, chew their resin,
play stories in the circle of birches where grass
stays green. And we drink from the hose.
The cool water is hard to gulp down,
but it lets us stay out with the flies and the noise,

the heat and the hum, the cactus and the drowsiness.
It teaches us our only enemy is the door.

my grandmother, a lake
Tyler Odeneal, Milwaukee

and she is not always this
body
to the brim with every
drink
waters rushing
currents pulling
wavy as they scoff, smirk
cool
just beneath the surface

man calls to her in the depths
finds her treasure dropped
bottomless
salmon birthing, giving her up as
sacrificial as every daughter that heard
her name on his tongue

sisters gone, given as other rivers
flowed, one with other gulfs
they cannot
will not reach for her

she sits cool at the bottom
warms her interior at winters
granting temperament hotter than centuries past and present
    and fires started

even burning through waters purifying
every ounce of her

she winks at you through rain pouring
from eyes into her body
man snorts the whiteness of skies
goes fishing at other lakes
bodies spread as women and men
give him vermin, he eats
not of grandmother
bringing her this wake

invasive species fill the depths, swim
counterclockwise, break the flow of
fish granted by generations swimming away
upstream even as I toss my net
or scarcely cast rod instead
this body gives me
love wisdom chaos
resentment come to know myself
say, of man, this body hurts still

drown in her, drown momentarily
she gifts me the surface
hands full of fish taken
her cool
waters wash our feet at the shore

A Line Meant *I have been thinking a lot about how water informs so much of who and how we are, how the spectrum of its temperatures—hot or cold or somewhere in-between—are akin to human temperament, in that they affect the world differently. Even the coldest of waters hold healing powers. Water is essentially passed down to us. It is in our blood, our DNA. I've started to think about how our ancestors near and far gifted us water, and water as metaphor: bodies of water and how they might parallel physical bodies, the power and complexity of women's bodies, the Black body.*

Untitled
Joseph Cook, Oregon

So I sip. Taking it day by day.
Moment by moment.
Not becoming overwhelmed.
Not rushing the process.
I once heard patience builds progress.

So I sip. Taking my time.
Tasting the waters divine.
There is no divide between my heart and mind,
Between my spirit and my goals,
Between the lust of this world and my soul.
I'm back in my flow.

So I sip. Taking it slow. Cherishing the taste, the nutrition,
Not regretting that soon I'll have to let go.
But I'll leave the cup behind with a small sign,
Take your time. Empty the noise. Quiet the mind.

Meeting at the River
Catherine Young, Blue River

Cool water is hard to gulp down. Take it slow—
remember to taste the snow
in it; try not to drown
in its sorrows
or joys.
Make the choice
to savor
this water
that travels the world
through time,
through each microbe
and child,
carrying rivers of tears.
Cupped in the hands
at a spring
or sipped from a tap,
this water was tasted
by your father, long gone,
your mother,
and all those they loved
going way, way back, before
you were born.
All you've ever been
is water. All
you will ever be
is in this stream.

Drink deep.
Remember.

 *Water is what I live, write, and think about. Long ago, I studied Fluvial Geomorphology—how water moves and shapes land. Now I believe water is everything.*

Untitled
Samuel White, New Lisbon

War chants reverberate thru the corridors of human hearts
Synchronized cries
Slicing thru racial divides
Oppressors sit
Skyscraper high,
Impervious to innocent lives
Being victimized,
Calculating the demise of the poor
While pouring out lies disguised as patriotism, as if I ain't got
    my own set of eyes
Pupils dilated, intoxicated with rage
tired of being hated
tired of defending my own space
tired of extending love
Only to be spit in the face
How much can a man take
As much as it takes
Be Patient
The cool water is hard to gulp down

Somehow Seems like Yesterday's Rain

RAIN Collective

*Half in, half out
it was supposed to be different, but it's all the same
enjoying the usual
I don't know what we are supposed to be doing
but something has unlocked a door.*

*No longer in despair, finally, a breath of fresh air
better than the old which makes space for
    creativity to expand
remember there is victory in silence
unable to escape the same mazes they can't stop
    themselves from building.*

Katrina Serwe, Campbellsport
Charles Payne, Madison
Ruth Markworth, Sheboygan
Esteban Colón, Kenosha
Angela Hoffman, Jefferson
Lisa Vihos, Sheboygan
Paxton Evers, Ashland
Gorden V. Pemrich, Racine
David Kilgore, Racine

Retirement
Bruce Dethlefsen, Westfield

it's raining right now
somehow it seems like yesterday's rain
somehow exactly the same
the very same rain
as rained yesterday

this rain coming down
is yesterday's rain
exactly the same
the same exact rain
as came yesterday

this rain
this rain
the same
the same
this very rain

rain
same
rain

That time Lily left Marshall to follow her dreams of being an artist
Charles Payne, Madison

I don't know what we are supposed to be doing.
I don't know why we are doing it today, Marshall.

Cumulus clouds cry tears of butterflies, and June bugs go
splat on windshields. Our sky transforms from green to gray.

I stand there in relief rainfall, listening to what heaven
has to say, burdens of a polluted atmosphere covering up

desires I have to be with you, my admiration forecasted through
weather apps issuing freeze warnings on clear and calm nights.

I think that I want to be with you! But
they say Lilys can survive without human interaction or touch.

In the hit American sitcom, How I Met Your Mother, *lead character Lily is happy with lead character Marshall, but a pregnancy scare and the opportunity of an art program in San Francisco have her questioning her choices. In the end, Lily breaks up with Marshall to head to San Francisco and pursue her artistic dreams, leaving him absolutely heartbroken.*

creative wash
Katrina Serwe, Campbellsport

somehow

    the stone-gray sky with pearl-edged clouds brings me clarity
    it

    lights the edges of these hills and fields and trees which seem

    to press the details of this place further into my memory
    like

    the blueprints of the house my husband built connecting
    yesterday's   structure with a new addition that holds out
    the rain   better than the old and makes space for creativity
    to expand

A Line Meant

This phrase sits happily in my mind. It makes me think of the storms I've weathered and how my life feels peaceful in their wake. It has been a gray sky week, but I have been enjoying every minute of it. The monochromatic landscape helps me see the shapes of things—the details of the tree trunks and branches, the shape of the land—and gives me space to let my mind settle and see my inner world with greater clarity. This mental space is complemented by a new addition we've added to our home, as now I have physical room to write and paint and dream. This poem reflects this "wash" of gratitude for space to welcome in creativity. It is not fancy and full, but the opposite—simple and sparse, like the elegance of a gray day or a gray watercolor wash.

Like Yesterday's Rain
Gorden V. Pemrich, Racine

When it rains, warm in the summer
Children and young adults play outside, enjoying the usual.
As a person gets older, walking in the rain
Becomes uncomfortable and to be avoided
At all costs. "Messy," they say.
The other day, an old man had the opportunity
To walk in warm summer rain.
He chuckled as he watched the children play
And frowned as the middle-aged rushed by
Holding umbrellas.
Pausing, he looked at himself, drenched.
As he started walking, he heard his shoes squishing.
Smiling, he said to himself,
"This feels like yesterday's rain."

Somehow, Seems like Yesterday's Rain
David Kilgore, Racine

Another day I rise, my head held high, staring at the sky, eyes peering through the sunshine, still unable to comprehend life and all of its pain, and why, somehow, it seems like yesterday's rain. Wet, drenched, bogged down, beaten to the ground, yesterday's rain left its mark, etched and stained, deep within my heart like a river cascading through the mountains, carving its way to the ocean. And like an explosion, everything is in disarray. Yet somehow, it seems like yesterday's rain. Memories so cold they freeze the soul—instant hypothermia, shivering and shaking but never breaking. Unable to breathe, I fall to my knees, eyes closed and losing control.

I ask the creator, PLEASE, help me understand the path to be a better man, to comprehend the difference between a foe and a friend. Open up my eyes, so I can see all of the lies and deceit before me. And as I bow my head with guilt and shame, somehow, it seems like yesterday's rain. And even though yesterday's rain was tragic, like magic, everything is changed. From hopeless to hopeful and dark to light, yesterday's rain has brought forth new life, and the opportunity to make things right. No longer in despair, finally, a breath of fresh air.

In the Bough of an Anxious Frenzy

FRENZY Collective

somehow we all survived.
I regret waiting to unleash myself,
bombarded by life's madness
I saw little twigs of inspiration resting,
a joyous calm, a quiet confidence
because I'll mess around and tell the truth.
darkness rises once more and I accept it, greedily,
*   with open arms,*
vulnerable, grabbing a morsel.
we are different but share so much the same.
daybreak shrugs off night sweat shudders,
smoke smells different
but I know I need to heal me.

Ruth Markworth, Sheboygan
Michelle Price, Eau Claire
Sidney Mitchell, La Crosse
Katrina Serwe, Campbellsport
Erin Schneider, La Valle
Lucy Tyrrell, Bayfield
Robert Patterson, Kettle Moraine
Fontaine Baker, Winnebago
Samuel White, New Lisbon
Darius Ali Williams, Stanley
Kristian Zenz, Milwaukee
Joseph Cook, Oregon

American Happiness
Nikki Wallschlaeger, Viroqua

Donna hasn't been herself lately, and her manager's having a fit. Jonah called crying this morning, George lost his wits again over something minor, Mildred says it's been years since she felt anything but guilt. Allison cuts herself because God said she's a sinner, Michael sulks on the couch refusing to make dinner for the kids. Omar is so angry. Angry all the time. At the holiday party, Heather makes her entrance, already trashed on wine. Tina sighs like a prophet in class, Imani is sobbing about her past to therapists who don't get it, as Roland freaks out for no reason on a cashier at the theater. Veronica is so bored she may as well be dead, wedded to a man she cannot love. Stuart has an awful opinion about everything. I mean, *everything*. Yusef's words sting everyone around him like a bee with bad knees. Larry buries people's pets for a living. Louise left her family at the Badlands and took off for Vegas. Dan ran. He just ran and ran, with nothing, into the woods. Grace shook her parents off and got cozier with their goods. Eleanor's favorite social activity is calling the feds on "suspicious" people when her daughters aren't occupying her time. Marianne, the respectable daughter, is demanded to grow a spine. **In the bough of an anxious frenzy**, MacKenzie cancels the seminar, goes to the bar instead. Terrance's permanent mood is brooding, and everyone hates him for it, especially his teachers. Esperanza got hassled at the park for sparking a blunt, even though it was in a decriminalized state. Freckles the cat actually came back, but he was still a miserable feline. Annabelle doesn't know the first thing about leaving: the distant dream of a tree living on top of a mountain.

Patricia is numb all the way to her lungs; they stole her voice when they took her son away. Eddie, on the other hand, is hell-bent on owning everything. He sees a community of poor folks and he gets the machinery ready. Jeri, the street mime, is unable to find a way out of the box they put them in. Glen drives everyone nuts when he sings. And did you hear about our girl, Heaven? She got on an international red-eye and was never seen again.

On So Many Levels
Fontaine Baker, Winnebago

Pull me into your everything,
Don't hide a thing.
I want your messiest messes,
Your greatest core essence.
Let us compare our worlds,
Share our hidden pearls of treasure.
Let us measure our paradigm of life,
Not in the bough of an anxious frenzy,
But swinging from wrong to right.
Let us entice to invite perspectives,
Reflecting upon our unique stance
As we intertwine and dance to a rhythm of two,
Sharing some of me, lending some of you.
Let us mine fields of matter,
Peeling back layer and layer of our respective existences,
And with persistence we will discover,
We are different but share so much of the same.
I experience love like you,
As I know you've experienced pain.
You hold on to things in your mind,
I store them in my brain.
So let us grab our shovels,
And dive deep into the grain.
We are the same on so many levels
From extraordinary to plain.

November 17th, 2016
Sidney Mitchell, La Crosse

Smoke smells different
when it's your own
belongings
burning

 *This is from the moment when I felt the most anxiety and helplessness of my entire life.*

Untitled
Erin Schneider, La Valle

Among the smells of fresh-baked bread and floor polish,
my grandma was slow to rise.

Bewildered by the hairpin turn
that Her son, my Uncle, took,
she thought, he must not be having a good day.
Jolted, she prayed aloud,
a sense of impending fracture needling her bones.
My uncle lunged first at His sister, my Aunt, whom he pushed
    out the door.
He turned, he bolted, he shoved his crying niece aside,
one of many undone,

and moved toward his mother's hip.
He recalled once being lulled to sleep on that very hip,
washed, diapered, fed, loved. How is it, then,
his nightmares had turned into daylight?
Grandma feigned first, then fell into a resinous pile.
On the tile, in the wake of wafting bread and Pine-Sol, the
    situation grew viscous.

Grandma, stuck in the shocked silence,
made sense of being fleeced
by the boy she'd brought to life and not to greed.

The police arrived, somehow we all survived.
My grandma's grief was to be nursed

as a ward of the state.

And in the bough of this anxious frenzy,
I mourn the broken limbs of family trees, and the desperate pleas of men.

A Line Meant

This prompt took me first to balsam fir, then to a poem I had revisited a few years ago, when I was at a low point. Somehow, firs make me feel alive. The line "bough of anxious frenzy" helped me climb into a family history of depression, which currently has culminated in an unfortunate event. This poem is a way to come to terms with childhood memories of a favorite uncle, whose kindness and humor I remember with compassion. The poem has also helped me make sense of the surreal end that befell my Polka Hall of Fame grandmother, who loved and raised eleven kids and died at ninety-eight years old in 2022, a ward of the state because of elder abuse from her son. It has also made my aunts and uncles have to choose who they believe: my uncle, or my aunt and cousin. It makes me sad, and, well, this poem helps a little.

from the boughs tossed in anxious frenzy
Lucy Tyrrell, Bayfield

snow falls in drifting veils
in the windswept woods
once visible, now after midnight
full moon obscured, Orion clouded over
dizzying flakes scatter the beam
of my Petzl headlamp
through the white, I strain to see
my dogs pulling in their traces
wind sways the limbs
branches wildly scratch the sky
all around, trunks creak, groan
eliciting my fear of toppling trees
along the way I stop the team
feed snacks of butter, frozen meat
tend to their feet, their precious feet
remove ripped booties, finger off ice
again, I stand on the runners
we advance into the swirling snow
miles ahead on this winding trail
lies the sweet light of the checkpoint
in the challenge of wind and white
so much respect for these huskies
proud to witness our resolve to press on
a joyous calm, a quiet confidence
beneath the boughs tossed in anxious frenzy
a catch at my throat for my running dogs

A Line Meant

I participated in the Midnight Run sled dog race one mid-February with my eight Alaskan huskies. During our forty-six-mile night run to the checkpoint in Chatham, the clear night, with the moon and Orion giving us a sense of direction, became a windy, snowy challenge. The experience seemed to match this prompt perfectly.

A Bouquet of Regret
Kristian Zenz, Milwaukee

In the bough of an anxious frenzy, I walked though those black doors,
and I thought I knew something. I didn't know much at all; perhaps I knew nothing.
I entered the flowered field named for a soldier as an egotistical fourteen year old, and my fortunes were foretold.
Not so much in academic terms, or statistical remains—
It was that storm of social butterflies that hit me like a train.

My eyes would dart across the open room, looking for some kind of truth.
I couldn't focus on the blank spaces in the sheets, or the ground beneath my own two feet.
I was sucked into the black hole of a life destined with the goal of creating a bouquet—friends upon which my confidence could prey.

In the past, the one that first passed, my own path would tell me where to go.
But now I was stuck on theirs, feet on broken glass, and I spiraled into vertigo.
My passions wilted like flower petals in the winter, and everything I knew to be gold
passed away and lost its glimmer.

I was a champion of the social construct, the architect of a menace looking to wreak havoc on many different souls.

In high school, you learn about the vast array of different genera,
the many souls that perpetuate these different populations. I learned about the dimensions of these genera whether I liked it or not. I regretted my genus, the way I
would hide my ways and shamelessly blend in the shadows that those species bled.

I began to think my current bouquet wasn't good enough, so I threw it away.
I nestled into the dense prairie and became wheat among the other wheat.
I wanted to chew on dirt like the rest of the lesser worth, and get my kicks from six
six

Feet below, it kept me grounded much more than before.
It took a trip to hell and back to pick up all the slack, and help me realize that in due time
I would reach a prime beyond other years' worth, and make all these troubles mine.

Then I was sixteen; gunned, geared, and mean, but I kept a straight face.
Butterflies wanted to pulverize and compromise my new bouquet;
I let them do it anyway.

In the past, not the first nor the last, my own path would tell me where to go.
But now I was stuck on theirs, not the worst nor the last, and I

spiraled into vertigo.
My passions wilted like flower petals in the winter, and every-
    thing I knew to be gold
passed away and lost its glimmer.

I regretted the artificial and the superficial
I resented the past principles to which I agreed
I regretted all the gas money I spent
To be sure my bouquet would survive the heat.

I regretted the way I looked at yesterday,
Hiding under bare trees and praying the rain
Would wash my seldom-seen solitude away.

I regretted the way I looked at my bouquet.
Hiding a variety of ultraviolet light in the fray,
It's fair to say the way it was sold was not to my taste.

I regretted the way I looked at my life,
Resenting all of my past mistakes.
I regretted waiting to unleash myself,
And to do away with my rotting bouquet.

Now I'm eighteen; gunned, geared, and mean, and I'm going
    places.
Butterflies tried to compromise and pulverize my new bouquet;
I don't let them do damage today.

In the past, in the times that didn't last, my own path would tell
    me where to go.
Now I'm locked onto mine, seizing the redefined, and escaping

clutches of my vertigo.
My passions have bloomed like flowers in the spring, and every-
 thing has returned to gold
and comes to life and falls back into sync.

In the bough of an anxious frenzy, I walked though those black
 doors
Thank god I knew nothing.

Silhouettes
Matthew McDowell, Waupun

The crows
All in a row!
D'alighting above as
bruised arms and the day
disrobed

The trees allied first
naked in their scene and sagging down
in the infant sounds and vibe greens
This baker's box shook from the hedges
their sulking shoulders joined
to brave the turning earth

Misunderstood
Robert Patterson, Kettle Moraine

I grew up in a place where being hard is more important than
    knowing the definition of a word.
Gettin' money is our favorite verb
and European luxury on chrome
is how we celebrate our achievements.
Some mistake the culture as misleading
misunderstand the aggression in our dealings
as justification to shoot an unarmed man in the back 7 times
and then take away his freedom.
The pursuit of happiness has 2 sides
both defined by perception and experience.
When you learn that your zip code
is one of the nation's smallest and most segregated cities
and leads the nation in incarceration
how would you define liberty?
If your perception and experience
is marred by impudence and ignorance
if your message is reckless
but you have the complexion for the connection
in the land of the free, home of the slaves
you can become the president.
My worldview is complex. A duality in singular form.
Kneeling during the anthem will bring a public lynching.
One nation divided against itself is the norm.
You don't want to see me in rare form, because I'll mess around
    and tell the truth.
They turned DOC numbers into dollar signs

the war on drugs was the tool.
They manipulate the masses so no one questions mass incarceration
as long as it ain't happening in your neighborhood.
We—the victims—remain faceless.
I know a man, who was once a boy with promise, sit in a room
with interrogators and tell the truth about a lie.
His mother was uneducated and didn't know the definition of
coercion so the judge gave him life.
The world IS black and white.
Lady Justice adorns a blindfold so she won't see
public officials keeping tally of wins and losses.
Children grow up without fathers because people
with fragile egos break and enforce the laws.
Our senators and congressmen are gangsters without impunity
redistricting voter maps and changing voting laws
that disenfranchise entire communities.
Would you preach unity if Tulsa was your community?

Untitled
Terran Kess, Redgranite

In the bough of an anxious frenzy
I find myself looking for you
Unanswered calls, your absence is present
wrapped in doubt and uncertainty
Whispering winds lick my ears
remnants of your voice sing happily
I am incarcerated by pain
yet freed by thoughts of your smile
When I need you most I look in the mirror
Buried in my eyes, you stare back with pride
I finally understand you're always alive

A Line Meant

In 2014, I got the earth-shattering news that my younger brother had been murdered. My father had moved quickly; my brother and I were only born three months apart. We looked so much alike everyone thought we were twins. I know you aren't supposed to have favorite siblings, but he was mine. Even after ten years, losing him has proven difficult to overcome. I move for both of us now.

And Holy Hot Damn, the World Is Suddenly Something Different

SUDDENLY Collective

We never saw this Coming.
I throw a stone into the pond and ripples make it
*   suddenly something different.*
A perfect pool for new children,
it made tears well up, crowding my sight,
their faces painted to hide their sad souls.
You tell me of past day trips, names of hotels,
*   events,*
the library of ancient thinking.
I wonder what he uses to keep them clean.
The world doesn't change, until it does.
Now I go to sleep feeling fulfilled.

Sue Blaustein, Milwaukee
Ruth Markworth, Sheboygan
Patrick Fogarty, Wausau
Angela Hoffman, Jefferson
Jeffrey McAndrew, North Fond du Lac
Michael J. Garvin, Milwaukee
Matthew McDowell, Waupun
Joseph Cook, Oregon
Darius Ali Williams, Stanley
Marilyn Zelke Windau, Sheboygan Falls

Blue Bird
Nick Demske, Racine

And Love, let me tell you,
this blue was not moving.
It was small and feathered and
it had a beak and wings,
but it might as well have been a trinket
made of tin.
I walked over to it
and it did this:

nothing.
I talked to it,
tried to let it know
in a language it didn't speak
that I wanted to help it,
and then I took off my sweatshirt
thinking I'd use it as a net,
which even sounds terrifying to me,
really.
Because with the adolescent finch I caught *last* week,
when Dale and Christian were outside the library,
11 years old each and unsure whether it would fulfill them more
to protect it
or to kill it,
that bird was not having it
and did as much flying as it could—
which was very little—to avoid our joint attempts.
And while it proved pretty feisty,

we were three against one,
and I finally used some plasticware and a lid
to catch it for a few minutes,
before we could put it on a higher ledge
with more green and landscape,
where all the other adolescent birds seemed to be hanging out.
it is so hard to know
what the right thing is
what is the right thing
to do
when you are trying to help someone vulnerable
even though they have made it pretty clear
they are not interested
in said help
And this is why
I took off my sweatshirt
to use as a net
on little tiny blue bird guy, *but
what the heck,*
I thought first,
why not just try with my hands?
And I did.
And he was so still
it was as if he were dead
(but he wasn't)
And eventually,
with a little coaxing,
he was in my hands,
his tiny talons,
which were not talons at all
but were still sharp,

digging into my palm
ever so slightly, which reminds me now of James,
who at 3 years old
is already a champion of naughtiness in my library.
No man in his life, and a mother who's sweet but
guano crazy,
and though my desk is hundreds of feet from our main entrance,
I still know exactly when he comes in the building
because he screams "Nick! Nick!!! I want Daniel Tiger Neighborhood!!!"
or some other such DVD with talking animals.
I correct this behavior as best as I can,
but when I put my hand down for a low five after chastising him,
he always just grasps it and holds on
for as long as he can,
and it surprised me greatly for the first few times
but now I've come to anxiously anticipate it.
Yes, Love, I thought of James
when this fluffy azure jewel
dug what it had to hold onto things
into what I have to hold onto things,
these hands that sow snap pea seeds
and type e-mails
and on a good day, explore all of You.
And now I have a blue bird in my hands,
or a bird that's blue at least,
and I have no idea what to do with it.
I am an idiot.
Why do I constantly offer the world

things I don't actually have?
So I walk over to the garden,
figuring I can put it in a greener space,
a space where soil is underfoot
and worms are under soil
and maybe this little guy can feed himself
at this point.
Which means the worms will die,
which confuses me
because I am a vegan
and it's all too much,
so I just sit on the ledge
of a raised bed
and pet my new friend
with my finger.
I brush his wings
and I slick back his crown
and it's like I'm imagining it now
as I try to remember it.
How could this even have really happened?
I touched his beak, too,
and he stayed perfectly calm for it all
as if saying, "Of course! This was what we were planning today!"
And I'm talking the whole time,
telling him how good he's doing,
how brave he is,
and how pretty,
how much better life will be here in the garden
than out there, weirdly, in the middle
of a sidewalk.
And the robins are hopping around

and the killdeer are making a racket,
so I stand
and approach them a little bit more
and start soliciting them for help,
begging them to foster
my mysterious indigo friend,
my tiny little friend
so fragile.
And as I'm pleading with the killdeer
and explaining the situation
so they don't think I'm just some wacko
off the streets
BAM!
Oh crap!!!
Love,
that's when the explosion happened!
And I tell you no one could've been more shocked than me,
and I yelled at the top of my lungs
and even laughed—maybe insanely—
which made the people walking to work
turn and stare at the man
howling like mad in the garden.
My bluebird friend
burst into strong, confident flight
and dipped and soared and finally
alighted on a telephone wire,
and holy hot damn
the world is suddenly something different
and then I realized, Love,
that this super weird thing
I had held in my very own hands

—You, my sweet friend, who are now
too high for me to even try to reach—
I realized that You
were not what I thought You were.
No,
You weren't even *who*
I thought
You were.

Changes
Patrick Fogarty, Wausau

The world is the same, remains the same, will always be the same
People change? Yeah right, have you met my mother-in-law?
No matter how much I train my dog, she still says no
My economics class will continue to be boring
My family Thanksgiving will still be full of food and arguments
My mother will still be dead
The world doesn't change, until it does
People grow in love, grow in maturity
When people are low, others can build them up
People remarry and live long and happy lives
Parents stay dead, but you think on them with love and fondness rather than sadness.
My dog is a lost cause; she is cute though.

 *I've been thinking about recent changes in my own life, which have created not just a difference in the world, but a new world entirely.*

Too Much!
Sue Blaustein, Milwaukee

I say it once out loud, and then again.
Holy hot damn.
Holy, holy
hot damn!
The world
is suddenly different.

It's fun to say
and safely accurate.
The world
is different
every day.
(Somewhat,
if not completely)

But this isn't
fair. I know what
you meant.

We never saw this
coming.

A Line Meant

This poem is pretty light. "Holy hot damn" is fun to say, as there's a feeling that the speaker takes (or took) the suddenly different world in stride. I thought about how "suddenly" and "different" are different for each person, but I assumed (maybe totally incorrectly) that the poem was a pandemic poem, so I returned to some seriousness at the end.

Search
Michael J. Garvin, Milwaukee

Barefoot forced march
The innocent mind captured
The library of ancient thinking
A trap
Guided by the faithful
Into the gilded house of worship
Pass the collection plate
To receive the Eucharist
Cram for the exam
Hit the stacks
Up all night
For the sake of scholarship
Privilege and pampering
To dress for success
Ignorant of the suffering
Our neighbors endure
Money and prestige
The car the house the family
My highway
Of outright lies
Then one day
With eyes closed
And mind somehow awakened
The dreams exposed
Somehow now apparent
The lies become transparent
Power is a cannibal

And we are the feast
They assemble as theater
Performing the tribal dance
Pretending to act
They sit on their hands
They know it's too late
To save the planet we burn
Jump off into space
They wait for their turn
And with all the knowledge
They assemble to deny
What seems so apparent
We're all gonna die
They don't just plot escape
But scheme to control
Numbers in the streets
Armed and ready to roll
The knowledge is real
But contrary to the truth
We all learn too late
What has been within reach
The ancestral dream
Of a world so serene
We're taught to ignore
Taught to want more
I dug my own grave
With the words on the page
Read myself to death
And choked on my last breath

Untitled
Marilyn Zelke Windau, Sheboygan Falls

Some things I can't remember.
You tell me of past day trips, names of hotels, events
I don't know.

Was it because the kids were little
and I had too much to deal with:

milk money, piano lessons, homework,
you being away on jobs in other states for months?

I reminisce about my father and sister not knowing,
their disengagement from long ago and from now,
dementia weighting their brains.

I know what I don't know.
Will I know ever?

Senior moments have set in. Is it because of the stress of the pandemic? Will these moments continue, become more prevalent? The world and my world are different these days.

Suddenly Something Different
Jeffrey McAndrew, North Fond du Lac

I throw a stone into a pond and the ripples make it suddenly something different.

I share a kind word and a friend's world is suddenly something different.

I share a smile and the energy in the room is suddenly something different.

I take a political stand and it can make society suddenly something different.

 *I've been thinking about how one person can make a difference.*

Psalm 1
Renee Lynn Glembin, Milwaukee

All across this nation,
this continent,
the world,
perceptions are
shifting.
The voiceless,
no longer silenced,
are rising
to speak,
demanding to be
heard,
waiting to ascribe to that
vast
holy motion
notion
that we
are all one—
not hypothetically, no,
but
unequivocally.
We breathe the
same air.
We pump the
same blood.
We implore the
same god,
though we call out

different names
to summon
her.
We hinge on
greatness,
yet fall to
our own ignorance
and
intolerance.
We flounder,
we scramble,
we claw
our way
up
and
out.
Sometimes
we don't
make it.

Nonetheless
we exalt:
We belong!
We belong!
We belong!
The hallowed halls of herstory
will remember this era of
Awakening
and call it
Blessed.
We have arrived.

Join together to
hold hands
and
look upon what
we have created
together
and
breathe in
a deep
cleansing
breath
and
whoosh out
the pent-up poison
of the generations
before us
and
exclaim as one
humanity:
Holy hot damn,
the world is suddenly
something
completely
different!

I woke up before dawn one morning and wrote this into my phone. I am generally not an optimistic person, so it must have been messaging from a better angel :)

Roots Are Tough as Dreams

ROOTS Collective

*i was just sitting in a dark cloud and now it's got
    light in it
the more I think the more I need peace
dangerous like a lethal weapon*

NJ, Wauwatosa
AW, Wauwatosa
LT, Wauwatosa

Field Guide
Margaret Rozga, Milwaukee

Here underfoot, an oak seedling
Looks at first like another weed
Or like the grass everyone steps on
But its **roots are tough as dreams**
Its stem smooth and resilient as silk
Its history a lesson in how to burl.

How to come up from underground:
Discard the tough outer shell.
It protects the heart, but invites

Squirrels. Allow instead oak-spun stories
To rise from womb in a web to the sky
Imagine what I could with such fierce will.

My Poem
NJ, Wauwatosa

like a dream, i don't like to do this. please help
can't stop. why not? because they said
if i stop i might get in trouble and get put in my cell
for not doing it
got to get my grade up. please help. can't fail
got to get done so i don't got to do this anymore

how I would dream when i started to grow up
wanted to do this and that, and now look
i ended up in a dark cold place where i can't see my family
where i can't be free or where i can't play with my friends
where i can't ride my bike

roots are as tough as my dream. i wish it could take me place to
    place
like i never did
my dream. it's long gone
when i started to grow up, to be in dark crowds with bad people
i was just sitting in a dark cloud and now it's got light in it
i run through it all day long
i wish i could leave it, but it keeps following me. why does it?

black clowns want me. i'm already in, one of the clowns
please stop chasing me. wonder why it keeps chasing my dream
    away
probably because it don't want me

to be what i want to be
or how i grew up and wanted to be.

Dedicated to Ms. Dasha
LT, Wauwatosa

She speaks with bravery, strength, and truth
She could go speak to big crowds but yet she chooses you
She's a teacher, a speaker, and so much more
If she charged for her poems she could help the poor
She went out of her way to come speak to us
For the time she's here, our worries turn to dust
Ms. Dasha, Ms. Dasha, Ms. Dasha
We enjoyed your presence
that was gifted to us
a present, but
dangerous like a lethal weapon
I know I'm not the only who got the message you're sending
Thank you for your time and blessings
Thank you, thank you, Ms. Dasha

Throwing Ropes
Cristina M. R. Norcross, Oconomowoc

My mother, my grandmother,
my great grandmother,
me—
as women, we have all buried our feet,
planted the roots of self
in the hopes of growing,
moving into meaning,
becoming our own terra firma.

With each generation,
hope filled tea cups.
The silent promise of better
rushed inside our ears,
a hurricane without sound.
We held our collective breath,
thinking that the weight of a womb,
at the very least,
belonged to our monthly burden
of pain and moon cycle.

I was planned,
pushed through the canal
of tomorrow
with the full knowledge
that my new day would bring
brighter ones for others,
but only if those, too, were chosen.

My fallopian hands did not obey function,
turned away from giving me the high five.
I had to step outside,
reach into the petri dish,
bend nature.
Eyes wide open,
the test tubes were my choice.
I gathered them,
wrote my name on stickers.

I had peace knowing that
emptiness could have been my choice.
Fullness could have been my choice.
Letting go at a not right time
could have been my choice.

The women of today and tomorrow,
who have no choice,
have been thrown to the back of the boat,
to sit with ancestors,
swaying with the waves,
at the whim of those who would reframe,
rewrite everything so hard-earned.

But my roots are tough as dreams,
may they grow, spread, tangle to survive,
throwing a rope of rescue to today.

Roots
AW, Wauwatosa

Roots are as tough as dreams
They make me think of themes
I think of the ocean
I hear people scream
I lie on my side
And think of my dreams
The more I think, the more I need peace
Rainy days, it rains on my feet
The stars shine, and I wish for better dreams.

A Canvas Full of Ocean and Song

CANVAS Collective

I stole the night
singing a beautiful creation
while sandpipers poked and probed

A mural of cosmic mysteries
rising to breath
Your gunmetal shades lay there too
salty charm and grief-speak
the small grains of stories we tell ourselves
the plink of the wind chime
and all who sink in the vastness of its depths

Fontaine Baker, Winnebago
Alfonzo Washington, Plymouth
Christy L Schwan, Cedarburg
Darius Ali Williams, Stanley
Diane Wirtham, Dodgeville
Shelly Conley, Milwaukee
Ruth Markworth, Sheboygan
Angela Hoffman, Jefferson
Lisa Vihos, Sheboygan
Jim Landwehr, Waukesha

From a Door Worth Opening
Destinny Fletcher, Milwaukee

There is a door with a light seeping through unscathed
A door never so ajar
Count the blessings in our cups
Pour them out until they are half empty
Maybe there is freedom behind her tongue
A war path beneath her toes
A grip between her nose
She is a woman with her light shining through
Awaking at the grasp of no man, at the words "I can"
Woman be a powerhouse
A light bulb during a blizzard storm
A canvas full of ocean and song
A portrait in the sun
A woman
In the doorway, she has found the fight
Carrying souls of those who have fallen beside her
Protecting her
Hinges at the neck
Bleeding in her silhouette
Has carried the children of the damned and unwanted
Been a body for hauntings
Woman
Doorway to another unsung hero
But she still seems to have
The sun

Sand Etchings and Pesos
Joshua Wells, Wausau

We live to tell stories, dream to tell visions,
Because with a word, everything is different
Than yesterday, than a lifetime ago.
Sketchings on sky-blue canvas, moveable as ocean waves,
They keep washing away sand etchings.
Yesterday that salt-cool water was hard to gulp down,
Found its salty burn too much,
Too many ice shards,
Too much noise … or too much silence to swallow.
Like romance in remembrance,
Ending without regret's sharp ache.
What passion sounds like
Rising higher than those waves,
Discovering visions toward
what I was meant to be!
Price tags on flame,
Today that ocean turned sweet.
Today that canvas was colored in murals
And a million graffiti stories,
Because we were created to tell them,
To hold them in hugs and embraces,
Pesos spent to live on poetry.
Because in those stories, pieces of others,
We find pieces of our own.

When We Were
Darius Ali Williams, Stanley

The world was old when we were young. The light we brought was new and exciting. We exemplified everything that was before, now lost in the ethos of time. We were tiny things of no particular matter, yet we were everything the world needed in that moment—a blank slate, ready to be filed with all the glories, wonders, and immense depths of pain the world had to offer to its chosen. Chosen, we were. The air, water, and ground itself hummed around us. We felt its pulse, marveling as we molded to it our beck and call.

We were a canvas full of ocean and song. A mural of cosmic mysteries, unexplored and free. We were young. We were young in every sense of the word. Young to the world, young to life, young to the point of naiveté—of what we were bestowed by the heavens. The days of ignorance we shall remember fondly, as we traverse the lands in search of the newness we lost, learning to have better discretion in all things.

In Another Language
Ruth Markworth, Sheboygan

Far below tinkered two-faced streets,
egg-yolk sky, narrow gestures of burlap sea,
everyday clatter drowns out, defeats
long, slow-pitched love songs' tumbling pleas.
Her barefoot language, languid, low,
tiptoes through walls, treading free
where below blue whales sing
dialects of love-salty charm and grief-speak.
But in her mother tongue, not so polished,
she sings the same song, tumbling noises signal paths,
verses on starvation's edge starting slow,
following grammatical rules, fresh math.
Wrung out, haunted by what night reflections bring,
she knows why the blue whales sing.

She may weary of journey's struggle to belong,
but she captures shy hope, dreams of place,
of painting a canvas full of ocean and song,
of blue whales, flimsy kindness, tattered grace.

A Line Meant

Some of the refugees I support and work with have struggled physically and emotionally, missing homeland and family. However, they are determined to make a new life and embrace the elusive American Dream. Sometimes taking two steps forward and one step back, they remain tough, resourceful, gracious, and full of hope and gratitude. I am proud to call them dear friends.

Beach Walk
Christy L. Schwan, Cedarburg

Ombré tapestry of indigo and sea glass and crystal
sky, sea, surf, sand
blending, melding, melting
sandpipers poke and probe
focusing on crustacean breakfast
missing the symphony ebbing and flowing

 *Inspired by early morning beach walks along the Gulf Coast on an overcast day, really watching and listening to the world around me.*

Art Attack
Jim Landwehr, Waukesha

The piece breathed the artist's rage at me
all her self-defeating demons screaming at once
echoing lamentations that nearly killed the work
accusations defending her twisted beliefs
murmurs coursing from head to heart
that she would never be what she really could
yet here she hangs in Chicago, in living color.

The oils spread flat on a bed of cloth
rise to their intended denotation, taking form
giving life and breath to both their creator
and all who sink in the vastness of its depths
changing their lives in small but significant ways
shining proof that the artist had no right
treating herself the way she did.

A Line Meant

Like much of my poetry, this piece started as an idea and then took on a life of its own. I began with the intention of it being about a beautiful portrait in a museum. The raging artist then took it and made it about them. Who am I to argue?

Dive In
Shelly Conley, Milwaukee

A canvas full of ocean and song
God sings an inclusive anthem
With weaving waves and whistling winds
There is rhythm here
A sway that can rock you to peace
Spread your heavy tattered wings
So you can float here without fear
Painting pictures of effortlessness
With each breath

Grab your blood-red and beaten-blue hues
From the ocean floor
Your gunmetal shades lie there too
Grab your shades of sun rays from the brightness of the sky
The kaleidoscope of colors from schools of fish
Lie still and let nature take its course
There is a canvas full of ocean and song
A masterpiece waiting for you
To add your personal touch

Old Rhythms Find the Hands

RHYTHM Collective

No one prepares you for the letting go
Dreams ripped from our palms
between the dark and daylight
clawing fingers carving off scabs that refuse to heal
slicing through soil secrets beneath us
Make me sing those walkin' blues
New eyes see the morning

Cristina M. R. Norcross, Oconomowoc
Ruth Markworth, Sheboygan
Jessi Peterson, Eau Claire
Esteban Colón, Kenosha
Angela Hoffman, Jefferson
Lisa Vihos, Sheboygan
John Snider, Ashland

Manoominike-giizis
Kimberly M. Blaeser, Lyons

Ricing moon
when poling arms groan
like autumn winds through white pine.
Old rhythms find the hands
bend and pound the rice
rice kernels falling
falling onto wooden ribs
canoe bottoms filling with memories
new moccasins dance the rice
huffs of spirit wind lift and carry the chaff
blown like tired histories
from birch bark winnowing baskets.
Now numbered
by pounds, seasons, or generations
lean slivers of parched grain
settle brown and rich
tasting of northern lakes
of centuries.

Skipping Records
Esteban Colón, Kenosha

I
spent years trying to pull connections apart, let her superior
 grasp of reality burn my ears black, absolute zero candor.
Remained
lap-dog loyal despite the patting of my head, her refusal to lie,
 to pretend like this was anything else, like I wasn't the kind
 of companion to be discarded when a home that wouldn't
 have me was easier on the pocketbook
  till
new homes nursing knotted gnarled wounds led clawing fingers
 to carve off scabs that refused to heal, and I learned that
 limb was extra, not a missing part
a superfluous one best left behind, marching forth toward new
 tomorrows
  till
the inevitable day my phone rings, the pulling of a parachute,
 eyes unable to watch to let her fall freely, mind screaming at
 feet, to run while I prepare to catch her to nurse her, our old
 rhythms finding my hands.

The prompt sings of neglected joys and relapsed pains.
That's how it immediately struck me, and I ran with it.

The Children's Hour
John Snider, Ashland

Between the dark and daylight
When the wounds begin to flower
The tally of dead grows longer
For now is the children's hour
I hear in the Senate chamber
Sophistry like drones
While in lands across the seas
Only parents' cries and moans
Small cries and then a silence
Yet I know by their vacant eyes
That their father, warm in his study
No longer by their love surprised
The sergeant at his TV screen
Laughing with comrades there
Just another video game
Spreading grief and death everywhere
Do you think, Ol' Blue-eyed Jesus
Because we gather in your sacred hall
That your loving Father above
Will bless us and kill them all?
For Isaac lies upon the ground
Our knife poised high in air
We send our prayer to Heaven
"Dear God, don't stop it there."

Mouldwarp
Jessi Peterson, Eau Claire

Old rhythms find the hands of earth thrower—a dark plush
    cylinder of fur,
rough paddle hands, sharp claws built to cleave the earth,
to slice through soil secrets beneath us.
All winter she wanders deeper catacombs, only surfacing
as April rains bring up the worms.
She smells in stereo, tilling lawns for larvae,
fiercely harvesting her worm-weight daily.
I never mind the scribbled signature left behind
she and her kind will still be writing long after we are gone,
for as it is written, the humble shall inherit the earth.

Once Sweet with Aging Pears and Autumn Breezes

PEAR Collective

*Who knew all the right things to say at the right
 times
We search for answers that will guide us
just whispers of breath
Was it worth the trip around the seasons*

*We share a future and past
I'm not sure why I couldn't say a word but in that
 very moment there was a moment of silence
I listened, feeling
If only I could capture Peace*

*For now, I am content to witness
a haven of first kisses and secret longings
hands soft yet firm
in flames burn the remains*

*We broke, small stone in a windshield
and so the cycle continues*

Robert Patterson, Kettle Moraine
Brenda Wingard-Hayes, Grafton
Anthony J Machicoté, Plymouth
Ruth Markworth, Sheboygan
Katrina Serwe, Campbellsport
Yolanda Allen, Milwaukee

Still Life
Dawn Hogue, Sheboygan

His favorite sound
he always told us
was the lapping
slapping tongues
against water, the
pups drinking.

Our goblets gather
dust now, cobalt
blue glass without
purpose.

**And the room once
sweet with aging pears
and autumn breezes**
is still as death.

I cannot bear to
open the door.

Transformation
Kay Tallmadge Augustine, Milwaukee

Once sweet with
aging pears and
autumn breezes

In her nineties
she grew tart with
unripe plums and
wintry blasts
speaking her mind
no longer fearing the
consequences

I listened, feeling
both envy and
concern

As an older woman, I immediately thought of changes that may take place with dementia, eventually focusing on a transformation I witnessed in a friend, who shall remain unnamed.

Burnt Amber
Antoine Murphy, Mount Pleasant

I / heard it in the breeze
once sweet / with aging peers
amongst the crackling of / wrinkled leaves
we fall when we leave / what's left
just whispers of breath
a musical clef / in A minor
weather used 2 b minor
major during storms
we engulf the gulf
so we don't get engulfed
raking in life n times
of fallen foliage
bagged like rotten spoilage
we together cushion, the fountain of youth
fallen from trees / of ancestor-ies
dot com
dead of winter
ushered 2 the prom
as
life formed
in the back seats of black jeeps
homage 2 the gray hair of black sheep

This is what i heard. A story of seasonality n its correlation 2 humanity.

Once Sweet with Aging Pears
Anthony J. Machicoté, Plymouth

Be you those images that
flicker like flames across my heart,
singing the tender parts, where once
hope resided in numbers too
numerous to count?
You, once sweet with aging pears
and autumn breezes
now nothing more than tart ways
and stagnant air
keeping me from being exactly
who I always dreamt to be.
How do I reconcile the old and new
the you who once uplifted like warm winds
on sunny days in late May,
now nothing more than dreariness
and baskets full of emptiness?

Orchard
Angela Hoffman, Jefferson

An afternoon, the beginning of September
we walk the orchard rows
trees laden with Zestars, Ginger Golds and
pears, plums in their royal purple and blue
vines heavy with grapes.
Our granddaughter selects a golden globe.
We all take a taste.

Below the trees lie fallen apples
bruised, decomposing, decaying
wrinkling into something void of fullness.
I sense her pa, my husband
going through the motions
forgetful, distant, distracted.
Am I selfishly expecting him to be full
of attention for us, the sweetness, the wind
wanting him to be strong, alert
not soft, malleable?
Cheated, cancer picking him
time will not slow down, or replay
for him, for me, for her
for the end of summer is beginning, once sweet
with aging pears and autumn breezes.

Once Sweet with Aging Pears
Brenda E. Wingard-Hayes, Grafton

Once sweet with aging pears and autumn breezes
The tree drops its spent golden leaves
Onto the soil, steeling itself for inevitable winter slumber

The tree, tacitly satisfied with its sweet juicy pears,
Freely lets go
Of those golden leaves that slowly turn to dust

For those once-golden leaves that slowly turn brown
Return to nourish the ground
That will provide for next year's sweet harvest

And so the cycle continues

I have fruit trees in my yard, and have been a master gardener at a point in my life. I harvest fruit from those trees every year and am thankful for the bountiful years (as there are always lean ones). Gardening/growing food to eat in Wisconsin is a very humbling experience. I appreciate the silent work that a fruit tree does to provide fruit.

Unfurl, like Petals Longing to Bloom

UNFURL Collective

Buried under a forgotten horizon
blossoming without restraint.
The silly seed is so special,
an epiphany, a breakthrough.
Blurs of oblivion,
she twirls like a Sufi,
a commandment to bow.

Men swaddled it tight with loops of twine,
a spirit of wonderment as
bubbles tumble, race forward, disappear,
sashes and sills peeling paint

the saltiness of your ocean's kiss.
Perhaps they left as slowly.

Donnie Gilchrist, New Lisbon
Terran Kess, Redgranite
Angelica Munsell, Union Grove
Anne Drow, Wausau
Samuel White, New Lisbon
Joseph Cook, Oregon
Carmenetta Malone, Milwaukee
Jill Madden Melchoir, Green Bay
Ethel Mortenson Davis, Sturgeon Bay
Marilyn Zelke Windau, Sheboygan Falls
Ruth Markworth, Sheboygan
Darius Ali Williams, Stanley
Angela Hoffman, Jefferson

New Dimensions
Cristina M. R. Norcross, Oconomowoc

This winter heart you carry
longs to trace the outline of a wing.
Open yourself
unfurl, like petals longing to bloom.
New worlds await
behind that door—
that beaded curtain.
You are the opening
to the next dimension.
Color breathes here
hues of chalcedony blue
and stargazer violet.
Whatever your flickering heart
can imagine
it lives.
Let go of unwanted burdens.
Wings will appear
transparent, gold dust flutterings.
Your heartbeat pulses
to the rhythm of a new atmosphere.
You are building a new world—
where the sky is moss green
jasper stones vibrate beneath your feet
and all who open the door
are welcome.

This Year I Alone Went
Jill Madden Melchoir, Green Bay

Alone I went, I went alone
to the rollicking Christmas tree farm;
the saw was sharp, sharp was the saw
that tucked itself under my arm
I felled a tree, the tree now mine
and I cradled it there in the snow;
men swaddled it tight with loops of twine
and I stood it up tall once at home
The scissors were sharp, the tree held still;
I snipped bindings, and her branches unfurled
reaching for all the space in the room
let loose upon a new world.

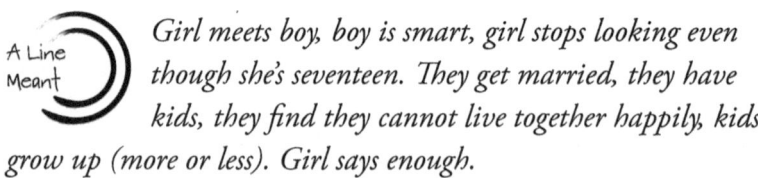

A Line Meant: Girl meets boy, boy is smart, girl stops looking even though she's seventeen. They get married, they have kids, they find they cannot live together happily, kids grow up (more or less). Girl says enough.

A Mirage
Carmenetta Malone, Milwaukee

Like petals longing to bloom
Stretching and protecting
Attracting and repelling
Polychromatic
Dangling
In the breeze
The gentle winds of the Eastern sun
A commandment to bow
One submission
Generously unselfish
Beautiful
As the bird of paradise
A mirage
Naturally exhilarating
Standing tall
On the tips of our toes
We, too, long to bloom
In the breeze
One submission
Beautiful
Standing tall

Untitled
Ethel Mortenson Davis, Sturgeon Bay

There is a painting
ready to be born,
pushing against the womb,
saying it is time—
now is the time—
to become, to be
a spirit of wonderment,
a pathway through
cherished clutter,
finally to be let loose
in our world, to lift us
        off our feet.

ACKNOWLEDGMENTS

My carceral work—like most of my endeavors—began with an invitation. Librarians Wendy Cramer and Sandy Rieckhoff contacted me about giving a poetry workshop and spoken word performance at the Racine Correctional Institution. That day was greater than I, the librarians, or the participants could have imagined; it was the start of a long and vibrant relationship. I've been humbled and honored to co-create a legacy with the participants, not simply deliver lessons. Nearly two decades later, I still volunteer as an instructor, coach, and program partner.

What I've most enjoyed about my tenure as a writing instructor has been the opportunity to curate community. Fontaine Baker and Daniel Scheidell were my earliest collaborators, again inviting me into fellowship. Fontaine came to the first workshop with kind eyes, an index of his writings, and focused expectation. Dan came to the second workshop with sign-up forms and follow-up assignments. He became the group's first proctor and forever named our series Prose and Cons. Peers, partners, and poets both. Our camaraderie has extended beyond workshop themes and prison walls. Dan was released and read at my inauguration as Milwaukee Poet Laureate. Fontaine has earned a doctorate degree and is whittling his time to release. As Wisconsin Poet Laureate, I gleefully wrote a character letter for his appeal campaign. They are the first of many comrades, collaborators, and brothers I've gained along this poetic journey.

Joseph "Heru" Cook writes poetry, fiction, essays, and has a recurring column with an outside community newspaper. He has resided in multiple facilities during his tenure with the Department of Corrections, and keeps me updated on his appeals and writing projects along the way. We talk about our manuscripts, philosophy, spirituality, and community health. The very first poems uploaded to the ALM project came from Joseph and helped create pathways of participation for incarcerated poets across the state. Thank you.

Finally, thanks to the Wisconsin Poet Laureate Commission, which has widened its capacity to accommodate this expansive and atypical initiative. They have offered editorial feedback for our poetry cohort and energetic support in sharing the project across the state.

POSTSCRIPT

If you are interested in adding your words to the A Line Meant collective, you can visit www.ALineMeant.org to submit a poem of your own. Whenever a new poem is uploaded to a prompt, everyone who has ever submitted to that prompt will receive a new email match for further collaborations, if so desired.

If you are without internet access, you can mail your poems to A Line Meant, c/o Mpact Communications, 333 W. Brown Deer Rd, G-721, Milwaukee WI 53217. Volunteers will upload your poems and return poem matches via postal mail. If you are interested in downloading ALM activity guides and curricula, or want to explore developing an ALM initiative for your state, please reach out to the editor at www.DashaKH.com.

We hope to continue growing this community endeavor for the indefinite future and, as always, it starts with the humble line.

www.ingramcontent.com/pod-product-compliance
Lightning Source LLC
Chambersburg PA
CBHW060529080526
44586CB00012B/680